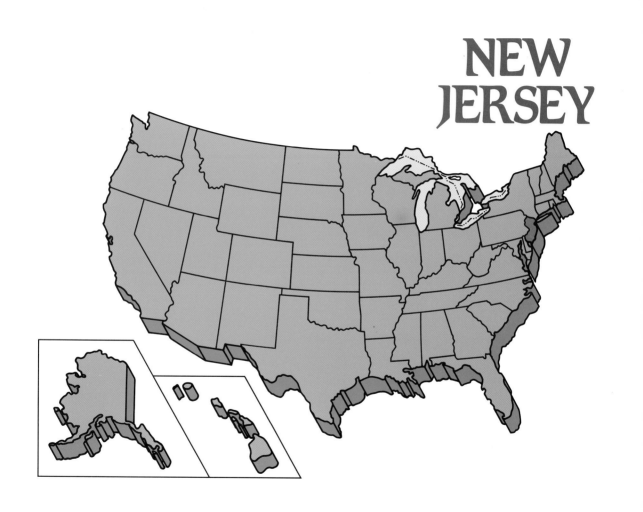

NEW
JERSEY

NEW JERSEY

Charles Fredeen

Lerner Publications Company

Cover photograph by Tony LaGruth.

The glossary on page 69 gives definitions of words shown in **bold type** in the text.

LIBRARY OF CONGRESS
CATALOGING-IN-PUBLICATION DATA
Fredeen, Charles.
　　New Jersey / Charles Fredeen.
　　　　p.　cm. — (Hello U.S.A.)
　　Includes index.
　　Summary: Introduces the geography, history, people, industries, and other highlights of New Jersey.
　　ISBN 0-8225-2732-4 (lib. bdg.)
　　1. New Jersey—Juvenile literature.
[1. New Jersey.] I. Title. II. Series.
F134.3.F74　1992
974.9—dc20　　　　　　　　92-13363
　　　　　　　　　　　　　　　　CIP
　　　　　　　　　　　　　　　　AC

Manufactured in the United States of America

1　2　3　4　5　6　98　97　96　95　94　93

 This book is printed on acid-free, recyclable paper.

CONTENTS

Did You Know . . . ?

❑ The first drive-in movie theater opened in 1933 outside Camden, New Jersey. The theater had parking spaces for 500 cars and showed two films a night.

❑ The first dinosaur skeleton ever discovered in North America was found in Haddonfield, New Jersey, in 1858. The fossil was a hadrosaur—a 30-foot (9-meter) dinosaur that had webbed toes, hundreds of teeth, and a beak like a duck's.

❏ The electric light bulb was invented by Thomas Edison at his laboratory in Menlo Park, New Jersey, in 1879.

❏ In 1877 the first interstate long-distance telephone call took place between New Brunswick, New Jersey, and New York, New York.

❏ Many people call Atlantic City the Saltwater Taffy Capital of the World. The candy became known as saltwater taffy after seawater drenched a taffy-vendor's stand in Atlantic City.

7

A Trip
Around the State

Millions of years ago, dinosaurs lumbered across northern New Jersey, leaving their footprints in the mud. Today, only fossils and skeletons remind us that these giant, three-toed animals once lived in New Jersey—a state that millions of people now call home.

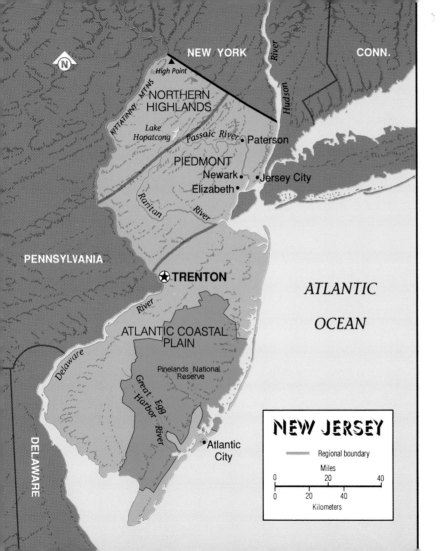

New Jersey is the fifth smallest state in land area in the United States.

Lying along the Atlantic Ocean, New Jersey is a Middle Atlantic state. Water defines all but one of the state's boundaries. The Hudson River and the Atlantic Ocean form New Jersey's eastern border. Across the Delaware Bay, which is off New Jersey's southern coast, lies the state of Delaware. To the west, across the Delaware River, is Pennsylvania. To the north and east is New York.

Three land regions cut across New Jersey. Two small regions—the Northern Highlands and the Piedmont—cover northwestern New Jersey. The Atlantic Coastal Plain, the state's largest region, extends over the rest of the state.

New Jersey's Atlantic coastline stretches 130 miles (209 kilometers) along the state's eastern border.

11

High Point, the state's highest spot, rises in the Northern Highlands region. The peak is part of the Kittatinny Mountains, which are located in the northwestern corner of this region. The Kittatinnies are part of a large chain of mountains called the Appala-

Fall colors brighten the highlands of northern New Jersey.

chians. This long mountain chain runs from Canada to Alabama. Formed more than 200 million years ago, the Appalachians are the oldest mountains in North America.

Rivers have carved deep valleys between these mountains and between the smaller peaks of the Northern Highlands. Some of the mountains are rich in minerals such as iron and zinc. South of the Kittatinnies is Lake Hopatcong, the largest of New Jersey's 800 lakes.

Southeast of the Northern Highlands lies the gently rolling Piedmont, a region covered by a **plateau,** or broad expanse of high land. Most of the rivers in the region form waterfalls when they drop from the Piedmont to the lower, softer soil of the Atlantic Coastal Plain. An imaginary line called the **Fall Line** connects these waterfalls. Early pioneers settled along the Fall Line because their boats couldn't travel upstream past the falls. Over time, the settlements grew into some of New Jersey's biggest cities.

A rainbow forms in the mist above a waterfall on the Passaic River.

People enjoy playing in the waves of the Atlantic Ocean.

The Atlantic Coastal Plain slopes gently eastward from the Fall Line to the Atlantic Ocean. Millions of tourists vacation on New Jersey's ocean beaches every year. People also come to the southern part of the region to hike in the Pinelands —an area of winding rivers and forests of dwarf pine and miniature oak trees.

Many rivers cross New Jersey, but the two most important are the Hudson and the Delaware, both of which empty into the Atlantic Ocean. Ships bringing goods from all over the world dock at harbors along both rivers. Like many other rivers in New Jersey, the Passaic, Raritan, and Great Egg Harbor rivers also flow into the Atlantic Ocean.

A farmhouse in northern New Jersey stands out against the snow. More snow falls in this part of the state than in southern New Jersey.

Ocean breezes cool sunbathers on New Jersey's seaside beaches in the summer. The average summertime temperature in New Jersey is 75° F (24° C), although it is cooler in the mountains of the northwestern part of the state. New Jersey's average winter temperature is 31° F (–1° C). Winters are coldest in the mountains, where about 50 inches (127 centimeters) of snow fall each year. **Precipitation,** which includes rain and melted snow, averages about 45 inches (114 cm) in the state each year.

Azaleas bloom in New Jersey in the spring.

Rain helps plants such as honeysuckles, mountain laurels, buttercups, and Queen Anne's lace grow in many parts of the state. The purple violet—New Jersey's state flower—is found in wooded areas.

Forests cover about 40 percent of New Jersey. Maple, birch, and yellow poplar trees grow in the northern part of the state, while cedars and pines thrive in the south. Deer, foxes, skunks, and mink roam the woods. Lurking in parts of northern New Jersey are two poisonous snakes—the rattlesnake and the copperhead.

Many types of birds and fish make their homes in and along New Jersey's rivers and coastal waters. Blue herons, ducks, and geese live in the marshy areas near the ocean. Clams, crabs, oysters, and lobsters live in the waters along the coast. And fishers are sure to find plenty of bass, pike, and trout in the state's many bays and streams.

Wading birds such as the blue heron *(above)* **and shorebirds such as the piping plover** *(left)* **can be seen along New Jersey's coast.**

17

New Jersey's Story

Scientists believe that people first came to North America more than 15,000 years ago by crossing a land bridge that once connected Asia to the North American continent. These people and their descendants are called Indians, or Native Americans. About 12,000 years ago, Indians made their way to what is now New Jersey, where they hunted deer, caribou, and mastodons—giant hairy elephants with big tusks and huge teeth.

By 1500 B.C., many different groups of Indians had settled along

North America's Atlantic coast. Those who lived in what is now New Jersey are called the Lenapes, a word meaning "people of the same nation" or "ordinary people."

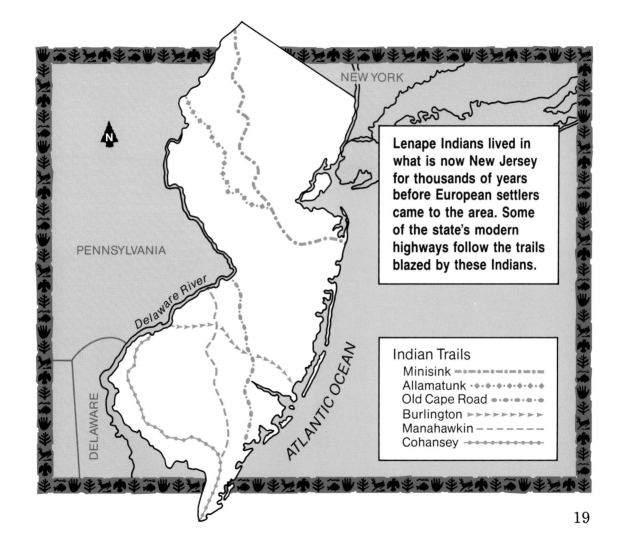

NEW YORK

Lenape Indians lived in
what is now New Jersey
for thousands of years
before European settlers
came to the area. Some
of the state's modern
highways follow the trails
blazed by these Indians.

N

PENNSYLVANIA

Delaware River

DELAWARE

ATLANTIC OCEAN

Indian Trails
Minisink ▬·▬·▬·▬·▬·
Allamatunk ◆·◆·◆·◆·◆·◆
Old Cape Road ●·●·●·●·●·●
Burlington ▸▸▸▸▸▸▸▸
Manahawkin ▬ ▬ ▬ ▬ ▬
Cohansey ●━●━●━●━●━

19

Using branches, the Lenapes built frames for shelters called longhouses. The frames were then covered with bark or grasses.

The Lenapes lived in small villages. Several related families usually shared a longhouse—a low, long shelter made from wooden posts covered with bark or grasses. Each family had its own space in the longhouse for cooking, eating, and sleeping. The Lenapes also built smaller bark shelters called wigwams, which housed only one family.

Lenape families depended on animals for many things. For food, the Lenapes fished and hunted deer and bears. The Lenapes melted bear fat to make a lotion, which protected them from sunburn and insect bites in the summer and kept them warm in the winter. They fashioned animal bones and horns into tools. Even fish teeth, sharp and pointed, were sometimes used to tattoo the Lenapes' bodies with images of animals.

Giovanni da Verrazano

In A.D. 1524, Lenape Indians living near the coast greeted Giovanni da Verrazano. Verrazano, an Italian navigator, explored the Atlantic coast and was the region's first European visitor. Almost 100 years passed before the Lenapes saw another European.

In the early 1600s, Dutch navigator Henry Hudson explored the Atlantic coast and then sailed up what is now the Hudson River before returning to the Netherlands. After Hudson's visit, the Dutch claimed much of what is now New Jersey, New York, Delaware, and Connecticut, calling the territory New Netherland.

The Dutch established trading posts along the Hudson and Delaware rivers, where they gave brass kettles, guns, and blankets to Indians in exchange for furs. The Dutch made money selling these furs in Europe.

Henry Hudson explored New Jersey's coast in 1609.

23

In 1629 the Dutch decided to set up a **colony,** or settlement, in North America. They started a system whereby a Dutchman could get a large piece of land in New Netherland if he agreed to take at least 50 people with him. Once in New Netherland, the landowner, called a **patroon,** was in charge of the people and the land.

Other Europeans were also attracted to New Netherland. Around 1640 the Swedes built two forts along the southern banks of the Delaware River. The Dutch, who wanted complete control in New Netherland, were not happy with the Swedish settlements. In 1655 Dutch soldiers took over the Swedish forts.

By this time, the British also had colonies in North America. King Charles II of Britain wanted to take over New Netherland to expand his North American empire. In 1664 the king gave the Dutch lands to his brother James, duke of York. James named part of the land New Jersey, after the British island of Jersey. The duke then sent soldiers to New Netherland to force out the Dutch, who proved to be much weaker than the British army.

In 1665 Philip Carteret *(center)* sailed from Great Britain to become New Jersey's governor. This painting shows his arrival at Newark Bay.

In other British colonies, European settlers weren't always able to practice their religion freely. When settlers in nearby colonies heard that New Jersey would protect religious freedom, many of them moved to the colony. Baptists and Quakers settled in eastern New Jersey. In 1666 Puritans from Connecticut moved to New Jersey and founded the town of Newark.

As settlers came to New Jersey, they brought deadly diseases such as measles and smallpox. The Lenapes had never before been exposed to these illnesses. Thousands of Indians died. Many others left New Jersey, heading west to what are now Pennsylvania and Ohio. About 24,000 Lenapes probably lived in New Jersey before Europeans came. Only 3,000 were left in 1702.

Palm Trees in New Jersey?

Early drawings of Lenape Indians by Europeans were not always very accurate. For example, the Lenapes didn't live in tepees *(background),* nor did they wear feathered headdresses.

Palm trees didn't grow in what is now New Jersey, either! The man who carved this woodcut in 1702 lived in Sweden and had never even been to America.

Like many people in the colonies, New Jerseyans were unhappy under British rule. The British government forced colonists to pay high taxes on paper, glass, tea, and other goods that came from Great Britain. In 1774 a group of New Jerseyans in Greenwich protested against these taxes by burning a shipload of British tea. Less than a year after the Greenwich Tea Burning, New Jersey joined the other 12 British colonies in a war against Great Britain.

During the American Revolution, the British army wanted control of two of the richest and most important colonial cities—New York and Philadelphia. Because New Jersey lay in between, many battles were fought there.

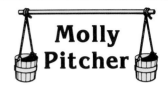

Molly Pitcher

One of New Jersey's most famous women was Mary Hays —better known as Molly Pitcher because of her role in the American Revolution. Molly's husband, John, fought in the Battle of Monmouth in June 1778. While John and other colonial soldiers were firing their cannon in the summer heat, Molly carried buckets of water to them, thus earning her nickname, Molly Pitcher. At one point, John was wounded and fell to the ground. Without hesitating, Molly took her husband's place and helped the soldiers fire the cannon. Many years later, Molly was given $40 a year in recognition of her service to the colonial army.

In the center of New Jersey's flag, two female figures support a blue shield. The woman on the right holds a horn filled with fruits and vegetables, which stands for agricultural wealth. The woman on the left carries a pole topped with a liberty cap—a symbol of freedom.

After many years of battle, the British lost the war in 1783, and the United States was born. On December 18, 1787, New Jersey became the third state in the Union after adopting the U.S. Constitution, a written statement of the country's laws.

New Jerseyans worked hard to rebuild their state, much of which had been destroyed during the revolutionary war. Transportation began to improve in the 1790s, when the state's first bridges were built. To cross rivers, travelers no longer had to rely on ferryboats, which were slow and unreliable.

Soon roads were improving, too. By 1829 New Jerseyans had built 51 **turnpikes,** or pay-as-you-go roads. A horse and rider, for example, had to pay one cent for every mile traveled—half a cent for the horse and half a cent for the rider.

In the 1830s, several railroad companies built tracks across northern New Jersey. The Camden and Atlantic Railroad made its first run across southern New Jersey in 1854, carrying passengers to a new resort, or vacation town, called Atlantic City.

By train, people from New York City and Philadelphia could take short, weekend trips to New Jersey's Atlantic shoreline.

Workers in this factory weave cloth. By 1860 New Jersey had become the sixth most important manufacturing state in the country.

As transportation continued to improve, New Jersey's industries grew rapidly. Trains brought iron ore from the state's northern hills to factories in Paterson and Trenton, where the iron was made into steel. The steel was then used to make locomotives and the cables for bridges.

Factories in Newark made just about everything—leather, clothing, carriages, knives, jewelry, tools, saddles, mirrors, and scissors. All of these goods, along with fruits and vegetables grown in southern New Jersey, were shipped to other states from the docks at Newark, Camden, and Jersey City.

Many of New Jersey's products were shipped to Southern states, where most people still made a living from farming. Many Southern farmers used slaves to do the work. But slavery was against the law in Northern states like New Jersey. Unable to settle their disagreements about slavery and other issues, the North and the South went to war in 1861.

A poster advertises for recruits in Newark, New Jersey, to join the Northern army during the Civil War.

Siding with the North, New Jersey sent 88,000 soldiers to serve in the Civil War. The state's industries boomed. Day and night, factories produced equipment for the war—locomotives, uniforms, blankets, tents, and rifles. New Jersey's railroads transported goods and troops to the South, where most of the battles were fought.

After the North won the war in 1865, railroad companies laid even more tracks across New Jersey. Towns and factories sprang up wherever the railroads went, and by 1876 most people lived within six miles (10 kilometers) of a railway. In fact, many rich people began to buy homes in New Jersey, taking the train to their jobs in New York and Philadelphia.

Many immigrants found jobs in New Jersey's factories, where they worked 15 hours a day, 7 days a week, for very low pay.

In the 1880s, people from Italy, Poland, Hungary, Greece, and Russia began leaving their homelands in large numbers, hoping to find a better life in the United States. Thousands of these **immigrants** came to New Jersey. Many took factory jobs in the state's northern cities. Others went to the southern part of the state to farm. Still others found jobs mining iron ore in northwestern New Jersey.

In 1890 New Jersey had close to 1.5 million residents. Immigrants continued to come to the state, and by 1915 New Jersey was home to almost 3 million people.

Many of these people worked in New Jersey's factories, which produced much of the equipment needed during World War I (1914–1918). Workers made bullets, gunpowder, uniforms, airplanes, and ships. Soldiers from around the country trained at Forts Dix and Merritt in New Jersey.

New Jersey's industrial power was called upon again during World War II (1939–1945). Factory workers made uniforms, ammunition, airplane engines, and

Soldiers fill out paperwork at Fort Dix. The camp was built near Wrightstown, New Jersey, in 1917 to train soldiers for World War I. The camp had 1,600 buildings and could house 70,000 people.

Many women in New Jersey went to work in factories during World War II.

ships. Scientists in New Jersey did some of the research that led to the manufacture of the first atomic bomb.

After the war, New Jersey's population grew, and many families decided to leave the state's crowded cities. People built houses outside the cities, creating communities called suburbs. To get to work from the suburbs, many people drove on a new highway called the New Jersey Turnpike, which was completed in 1952.

In the 1960s and 1970s, New Jersey tried to improve living conditions in cities by building giant housing projects like this one in Newark.

As New Jerseyans settled in the suburbs, they spent less and less of their money in the state's cities. Suburban residents, who were mainly white people, also paid taxes to their suburbs instead of to the cities. Cities had less money to support schools and to repair roads. As a result, New Jersey's cities began to decay. Businesses closed and houses and buildings started to fall apart.

Many black New Jerseyans, who could not afford to move to the suburbs, were angry about living conditions in the state's crumbling cities. Riots broke out in the black neighborhoods of several of these cities during the summer of 1967. More than two dozen people were killed in Newark, where the worst rioting took place.

New Jersey's government realized that something had to change. But to improve living conditions, the state needed money. So in the late 1960s, New Jersey set up a **lottery,** a state-run game in which people buy tickets to win prizes. The state also added a tax to items sold in stores. And in 1976, New Jersey's voters agreed to allow **gambling,** or betting on games, to take place in Atlantic City. The state uses the money it earns from these sources to build schools, office buildings, neighborhood centers, and highways.

10,000 B.C.   **A.D.1524**   **1609**   **1664**   **1774**   **1787**

Ancestors of the Lenapes come to New Jersey

Giovanni da Verrazano explores the Atlantic coast

Henry Hudson sails up the Hudson River

British army forces Dutch out of New Netherland

Greenwich Tea Burning

New Jersey becomes the third state

New Jersey's capitol building is in Trenton.

40

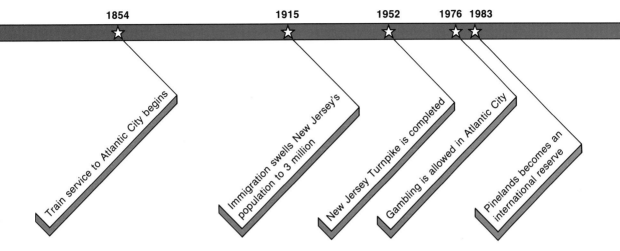

1854	Train service to Atlantic City begins
1915	Immigration swells New Jersey's population to 3 million
1952	New Jersey Turnpike is completed
1976	Gambling is allowed in Atlantic City
1983	Pinelands becomes an international reserve

Not all of New Jersey's problems have been solved, though. Many New Jerseyans are still very poor. And with so many people and industries, pollution is a big problem.

New Jerseyans are working to solve some of their environmental problems. In 1978 the Pinelands, a forested area in southern New Jersey, became a specially protected national park. And in 1983, the United Nations established this area as one of only a few international reserves, or parks, in the world. Working together, New Jerseyans can continue to set examples for solving problems.

41

Living and Working in New Jersey

If you've ever played the game Monopoly, you already know something about the state of New Jersey. Monopoly is a game about buying and selling property in Atlantic City—one of New Jersey's most famous resort towns. More than 30 million people visit Atlantic City each year. That's almost four times the number of people who live in the entire state!

With 7.7 million residents, New Jersey is one of the most populated states in the country. And because it is small, New Jersey is the most crowded state. On average, for every square mile in New Jersey, you will find close to 1,000 people.

New Jerseyans enjoy a parade.

Most New Jerseyans—about 89 percent—live in urban areas, or cities. Only California has a higher percentage of city dwellers. New Jersey's largest cities are Newark, Jersey City, Paterson, Elizabeth, and Trenton—the state capital.

White people make up 79 percent of New Jersey's population. Just over 13 percent of New Jerseyans are African Americans. Latinos and Asian Americans make up a smaller part of the population. Very few Native Americans live in New Jersey. Most of them left the state by the early 1700s, and their descendants now live in Wisconsin, Kansas, Oklahoma, and Canada.

New Jersey is sometimes called the Garden State because of the many flowers, fruits, and vegetables grown there.

Before factories were built in New Jersey, most people made a living from farming. Now only 1 percent of New Jersey's workers have jobs in agriculture. Gardeners in New Jersey's greenhouses grow millions of roses each year, as well as mums, geraniums, and lilies.

Throughout New Jersey, farmers grow fruits and vegetables such as tomatoes, cabbages, lettuce, potatoes, and sweet corn. Blueberries and cranberries are important crops from the Pinelands. Farmers raise dairy cattle in northwestern New Jersey.

About 20 percent of New Jersey's workers have jobs in manufacturing. Many of New Jersey's factories are in big cities such as Newark and Jersey City. The state leads the nation in its output of chemicals. Some of the chemical products made in New Jersey are medicine, shampoo, laundry detergent, and paint.

Food-processing plants in southwestern New Jersey package fruits and vegetables grown by the state's farmers. Other factories make computers, clothing, and medical instruments. The telephone in your house was probably made in New Jersey, too!

Most of New Jersey's workers—about 75 percent—have service jobs. Instead of making products, service workers help people. New Jersey's service workers include government workers, salesclerks, waiters, doctors, and agents who sell homes and office buildings. Workers at the Fort Dix military training camp have service jobs. So do the researchers who work in New Jersey's many laboratories.

Like the worker in this soap factory *(left)*, many New Jerseyans have jobs in industry. Some New Jerseyans make a living from fishing *(below)*. New Jersey's fishing industry earns the state about $60 million each year.

A boy builds a sand castle *(inset)* **along the Atlantic Ocean near Cape May, New Jersey. The Atlantic is also a popular place for boating** *(above).*

48

New Jerseyans have little trouble finding places to enjoy themselves. Along the state's coast, people swim, surf, and hunt for seashells. Boating is popular, too. Small boats take advantage of a sheltered water route called the Atlantic Intracoastal Waterway. Running along the Atlantic Coast from Massachusetts to Florida, this waterway is protected from the rest of the ocean by a string of islands and sandbars.

Atlantic City, one of the largest seaside resorts in the world, lies on New Jersey's southern coast. Stretching along the ocean, the city's famous wooden sidewalk—the Boardwalk—is lined with **casinos,** or gambling houses, hotels, restaurants, and shops. One of the best-known spots on the Boardwalk is the Convention Center, where the Miss America Pageant is held each September.

Sports fans go wild in New Jersey. Two professional football teams—the New York Giants and the New York Jets—play in the huge Meadowlands Sports Complex in East Rutherford, New Jersey. The New Jersey Nets swish the hoops on the complex's basketball court, while the New Jersey Devils pass the puck in the Meadowlands's hockey arena.

People looking for quieter places can visit Princeton University. Founded in 1746, Princeton is the fourth oldest university in the United States. Among the school's many historical buildings is Nassau Hall, which was the site of the U.S. Capitol in 1783.

History buffs touring the Hancock House in southwestern New Jersey see how early Quaker colonists lived. Walking in Monmouth Battlefield State Park, visitors can try to imagine the revolutionary war battle that took place at this site more than 200 years ago. In West Orange, faces light up at the Edison National Historic Site. Here in his laboratory and workshops, Thomas Edison invented the movie camera and the record player.

The New York Jets play the Indianapolis Colts *(facing page)* in New Jersey's Meadowlands Sports Complex. Many New Jerseyans also enjoy watching horse races *(above)* at Monmouth Park.

Bobcat

People are sometimes surprised to discover that New Jersey, which is crisscrossed by highways, has more than 50 state parks and forests. Walking along the trails that pass through High Point State Park, hikers might spot a bear or a bobcat. Visitors to Liberty State Park near Jersey City can look across the New York Bay to see New York City's skyline and the Statue of Liberty.

Hikers following the Batona Trail through New Jersey's Pinelands will walk through three state

New York City's skyline is visible from Jersey City, New Jersey.

forests before completing the 48-mile (77-km) wilderness route. And along the way, a visitor just might see the Jersey Devil—a legendary creature said to have the body of a kangaroo, the head of a dog, the face of a horse, the wings of a bat, the feet of a pig, and a forked tail!

To build roads and highways *(inset),* **workers often must cut down trees, which destroys forests** *(above).*

54

Protecting the Environment

About 8 million people call New Jersey home. Houses, shopping malls, hotels, restaurants, factories, offices, trains, cars, and buses meet the eye in all directions. As New Jersey's population continues to grow, developers, or builders, put up more houses and build more resorts and roads.

But overdevelopment happens when people build too much, causing problems in the environment. When trees are cut down to make way for new buildings and roads, animals lose a place to live and raise their young. New roads also bring in automobiles, trucks, and buses, which pollute the air with their exhaust.

In the 1970s, New Jerseyans decided to do something about overdevelopment in their state. They decided to preserve more than 1 million acres (405,000 hectares) of land known as the Pinelands (or the Pine Barrens) in southern New Jersey. From the story of the Pinelands, New Jerseyans know that they can work together to protect their environment.

The Pine Barrens tree frog
lives in swamps in the
Pinelands.

The Pinelands is an area of cedar swamps, forests of dwarf oak and pine trees, twisting rivers, and insect-eating plants such as the northern pitcher and the sundew. Animals such as the Pine Barrens tree frog and the bog turtle, which are in danger of becoming extinct, live in the Pinelands. In the central part of the Pinelands, cranberry and blueberry farmers harvest their crops. Small towns and historic villages dot the landscape.

Ever since white settlers first came to New Jersey, people have been trying to develop the Pinelands. At different times throughout the history of the Pinelands, people have come to farm, to cut down trees, to mine iron, and to tap water from the Cohansey Aquifer—a giant underground storehouse of fresh water.

Cranberries that grow in the Pinelands are an important crop in New Jersey. Only two other states grow more cranberries than New Jersey does.

Atlantic City once threatened to spread into the nearby Pinelands. But many New Jerseyans worked hard to make sure that wouldn't happen.

One of the most serious threats to the Pinelands was the growth of nearby Atlantic City in the 1970s.

After gambling was legalized in 1976, people rushed to the city to build hotels, restaurants, and casinos. New Jerseyans worried that Atlantic City would grow bigger and expand into the Pinelands, spoiling the land and polluting—or even using up—the water in the Cohansey Aquifer.

In 1977 a group of New Jerseyans formed the Pine Barrens Coalition to speak out against overdevelopment in the Pinelands. In 1978 New Jersey's government responded by passing laws to protect the water of the Cohansey Aquifer. That same year, the U.S. Congress established the Pinelands National Reserve—the first reserve in the United States. This means that government groups work to protect the land, animals, plants, and waters from the dangers of overdevelopment.

The Pinelands' winding rivers are great for canoeing.

Blueberries grow well in the Pinelands.

Some people are unhappy with the government's rules to limit development in the Pinelands. Residents feel that they no longer have control of their land. Others feel the environment has gotten worse since the Pinelands reserve was created.

Before it became a reserve, they say, few people knew about the Pinelands. Development wasn't a problem. But now, more and more people visit the area to picnic or camp. Some of these people don't always respect the land, dumping pop cans on the side of the road or damaging property.

But most everyone agrees that the Pinelands is a treasure. Located in the most populated region of the country, the Pinelands stands as the largest wilderness area between Boston and Washington, D.C. New Jerseyans are striving to keep it that way.

New Jersey's Famous People

ACTORS

John Amos (born 1942) is an actor from Newark. Amos played the part of Kunte Kinte in the TV mini-series *Roots* and starred as James Evans in the television series "Good Times."

Jack Nicholson (born 1937) is a well-known actor who has starred in many movies. He won Academy Awards for his performances in *One Flew Over the Cuckoo's Nest* and *Terms of Endearment*. Nicholson is from Neptune, New Jersey.

Meryl Streep (born 1949) of Summit, New Jersey, has appeared in many motion pictures, on stage, and in television films. She won Academy Awards for her performances in *Kramer vs. Kramer* and *Sophie's Choice*.

▲ JOHN AMOS

▼ JACK NICHOLSON

◄ MERYL STREEP

DOROTHEA LANGE ▼

ARTISTS & PHOTOGRAPHERS

Dorothea Lange (1895–1965) is famous for the photographs she took of families during the Great Depression. These pictures, published in newspapers and magazines, convinced people to support programs that would help needy families. Born in Hoboken, Lange traveled all over the world during her career, taking pictures in Asia, Africa, and South America.

Jacob Lawrence (born 1917) is a painter from Atlantic City. Some of his paintings, such as *The Life of Harriet Tubman*, are collections of 40 or more panels that illustrate African American history.

Alfred Stieglitz (1864–1946), born in Hoboken, was a photographer who helped establish photography as an art form. In 1903 Stieglitz started a magazine called *Camera Work*. Two years later, he started an art gallery in New York City, where he showed paintings, sculptures, and photographs done by promising American and European artists.

ALFRED STIEGLITZ ▶

ATHLETES

Franco Harris (born 1950) played football with the Pittsburgh Steelers for 12 years. Harris helped his team win four Super Bowls, and he ran more than 1,000 yards each season for eight years. The quick running back was born in Fort Dix, New Jersey.

Joe Medwick (1911–1975) played baseball with the St. Louis Cardinals. In 1937 he won baseball's Triple Crown by leading the National League in homeruns, runs batted in, and batting average. Medwick was born in Carteret, New Jersey.

◀ FRANCO
HARRIS

◀ JOE
MEDWICK

CHARLES E.
▼ HIRES

BUSINESS LEADERS

Edna Woolman Chase (1877–1957) was the editor-in-chief of *Vogue* magazine from 1914 to 1955. In 1944 she organized the first fashion show in the United States. Chase was born in Asbury Park, New Jersey.

Charles E. Hires (1851–1937) introduced his new soft drink, root beer, at the 1876 Centennial Exposition in Philadelphia, Pennsylvania. The inventor, born near Roadstown, New Jersey, patented his formula and began to sell the popular Hires Root Beer.

63

LEADERS & POLITICIANS

Alice Paul (1885–1977), born in Moorestown, New Jersey, was a leader in the fight for equal rights for women. Paul founded the National Woman's Party in 1913 and worked for women's right to vote, which was granted in 1920.

Woodrow Wilson (1856–1924) moved to New Jersey in 1890 to teach at Princeton University, later becoming the university's president. After serving as governor of New Jersey, he went on to become the 28th president of the United States.

◀ ALICE PAUL

WOODROW WILSON ▶

MUSICIANS

Whitney Houston (born 1963) has a voice that caught many people's attention when she was still in grade school. Her first album, released in 1985, sold over 14 million copies worldwide. Houston was born in Newark.

◀ FRANK SINATRA

▼ PAUL SIMON

Paul Simon (born 1941) was born in Newark. While in his teens, he met Art Garfunkel, with whom he performed for many years, creating hit songs like "Mrs. Robinson" and "Bridge over Troubled Water." In 1971 Simon began to perform on his own. His solo album *Graceland* won a Grammy Award in 1987.

Frank Sinatra (born 1915) has been a popular singer for over 50 years. Sinatra has also acted in more than 60 films, winning an Academy Award in 1953 for his role in *From Here To Eternity.* Sinatra is from Hoboken.

◀ WHITNEY HOUSTON

Bruce Springsteen (born 1949) was born in Freehold, New Jersey. In 1973 he started the E Street Band. With albums such as *Born to Run* and *Born in the U.S.A.,* Springsteen became one of the most popular rock stars of his time.

BRUCE SPRINGSTEEN ◄

WRITERS

Judy Blume (born 1938), of Elizabeth, New Jersey, writes books for adults and young people. Her titles include *Tales of a Fourth Grade Nothing, Blubber,* and *Tiger Eyes.* Many people like Blume's books because they use everyday language to tell about real-life situations.

◄ **STEPHEN CRANE**

JUDY BLUME ►

Stephen Crane (1871–1900) was born in Newark and became one of the most famous writers of his time. His book *The Red Badge of Courage,* which is set during the Civil War, tells of the horrors of war.

Mary Elizabeth Mapes Dodge (1831–1905) began her writing career after moving to Newark at the age of 27. Dodge is best known for her children's book *Hans Brinker, or, The Silver Skates,* which tells the story of a young Dutch boy who competes in an ice-skating race.

William Pène Du Bois (born 1916) is a children's writer and illustrator. Born in Nutley, New Jersey, Du Bois won the Newbery Medal in 1948 for his book *The Twenty-One Balloons.*

MARY ELIZABETH MAPES DODGE ►

Facts-at-a-Glance

Nickname: Garden State
Song: none
Motto: Liberty and Prosperity
Flower: purple violet
Tree: red oak
Bird: eastern goldfinch

Population: 7,730,188*
Rank in population, nationwide: 9th
Area: 8,722 sq mi (22,590 sq km)
Rank in area, nationwide: 47th
Date and ranking of statehood:
    December 18, 1787, the 3rd state
Capital: Trenton
Major cities (and populations*): Newark
    (275,221), Jersey City (228,537), Paterson
    (140,891), Elizabeth (110,002), Trenton (88,675)
U.S. senators: 2
U.S. representatives: 13
Electoral votes: 15

Places to visit: Discovery Seashell Museum in
Ocean City, Batsto Historic Village in Hammonton,
Double Trouble State Park in Berkeley, Edison National Historic Site in West Orange, Great Adven-
ture amusement park in Jackson

Annual events: Super Science Weekend in Trenton (Jan.), National Marbles Tournament in Wild-
wood (June), Barnegat Bay Crab Race and Seafood
Festival in Seaside Heights (Aug.), Sussex Air Show
(Aug.), Reenactment of George Washington's Crossing of the Delaware at Washington Crossing (Dec.)

* 1990 census

Average January temperature: 31° F (−1° C)   **Average July temperature:** 75° F (24° C)

Natural resources: soil, granite, sand and gravel, clay, greensand marl, peat, zinc

Agricultural products: roses, holly, milk, tomatoes, cabbages, peaches, blueberries, cranberries, eggs, cattle, hogs

Manufactured goods: chemicals, medicines, shampoos, lotions, detergents, paints, bakery products, telephones, lighting supplies

ENDANGERED SPECIES
Mammals—bobcat, eastern wood rat, fin whale, blue whale, humpback whale, black right whale
Birds—pied-billed grebe, bald eagle, Cooper's hawk, red-shouldered hawk, short-eared owl
Reptiles—bog turtle, Atlantic leatherback turtle, corn snake, timber rattlesnake
Amphibians—blue-spotted salamander, Pine Barrens tree frog
Plants—puttyroot, cuckoo flower, robin-run-away, elephant's foot, Aunt Lucy, meadow horsetail

WHERE NEW JERSEYANS WORK
Services—60 percent
  (services includes jobs in trade; community, social, & personal services; finance, insurance, & real estate; transportation, communication, & utilities)
Manufacturing—20 percent
Government—15 percent
Construction—4 percent
Agriculture—1 percent

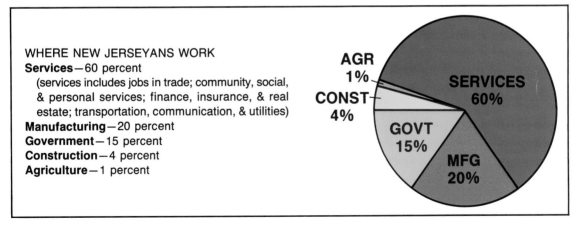

AGR
1%
CONST
4%
SERVICES
60%
GOVT
15%
MFG
20%

PRONUNCIATION GUIDE

Appalachian (ap-uh-LAY-chuhn)

Cohansey Aquifer (koh-HAN-see AK-wuh-fur)

Hopatcong (huh-PAT-kahn)

Kittatinny (KIHT-uh-TIHN-ee)

Lenape (luh-NAH-pay)

Monmouth (MAHN-muth)

Newark (NOO-urk)

Passaic (puh-SAY-ihk)

Paterson (PAT-ur-suhn)

Piedmont (PEED-mahnt)

Verrazano, Giovanni da (vehr-raht-SAHN-oh, joh-VAHN-nee dah)

Glossary

casino A room or building where people gamble.

colony A territory ruled by a country some distance away.

Fall Line A line that follows the points at which high, rocky land drops to low, sandy soil. Numerous waterfalls are created along this line when rivers tumble from the upland to the lowland. In the United States, a fall line runs from New Jersey to Alabama.

gambling Placing bets (usually money) on a game such as poker or dice.

immigrant A person who moves into a foreign country and settles there.

lottery A game of chance in which people pick numbers that they hope will match numbers chosen in a regularly scheduled drawing. Players pay a small fee for each numbered ticket. Winners cash in their tickets, sometimes for large sums of money.

patroon A man who was given land in New Netherland that he could rent to others.

plateau A large, relatively flat area that stands above the surrounding land.

precipitation Rain, snow, and other forms of moisture that fall to earth.

turnpike A highway on which a toll, or fee, is collected from drivers at various points along the route.

Index

Acknowledgments

Maryland Cartographics, Inc., pp. 2, 10; Alan L. Detrick, pp. 2–3, 13, 48 (right), 54 (inset), 58; Camden County Historical Society, N.J., p. 6; Toby Schnobrich, p. 7; Michael J. Kilpatrick, pp. 8–9, 11, 17 (left), 47 (right), 52, 54 (right), 60, 61; Tony LaGruth, pp. 12, 18, 53, 68, 71; James Mejuto Photo, pp. 14, 16, 48 (inset), 49, 50, 51; Saul Mayer, p. 15; Clay Myers, p. 17 (right); John T. Kraft, Seton Hall University Museum, p. 20; Library of Congress, pp. 22, 23, 32–33; Special Collections and Archives, Rutgers University Libraries, pp. 25, 36, 64 (top right); The Library Company of Philadelphia, p. 27; *The American Revolution*, Dover Publications, Inc., pp. 28–29; Newark Public Library, pp. 31, 34, 38, 64 (top left), 65 (bottom right); The Bettmann Archive, p. 35; National Archives, p. 37; Joseph Moore, p. 40; Claudio Ferrer / Tony Stone Worldwide, pp. 42–43; Jeff Greenberg, pp. 44, 47 (left); William W. Hawkins, pp. 45, 56, 59; Betty Groskin, p. 57; Hollywood Book & Poster Co., pp. 62 (top right and left, bottom left), 64 (bottom right and center), 65 (top left); Oakland Museum-Dorothea Lange Collection, p. 62 (bottom right); *Dictionary of American Portraits,* pp. 63 (top right), 65 (bottom left); Pittsburgh Steelers, p. 63 (top left); Cleveland Public Library, p. 63 (bottom left); The Procter & Gamble Company, p. 63 (bottom right); Independent Picture Service, p. 64 (bottom left); UPI / Bettmann, p. 65 (top right); Jean Matheny, p. 66.